LaMeNtInG My FaIlUrE tO LeArN HoW tO TaP DaNcE

And Other Missteps

Joan Wiese Johannes

Copyright © 2023 by Joan Wiese Johannes

All rights reserved.

Printed in the United States of America

Water's Edge Press LLC
Tucson, AZ
watersedgepress.com

ISBN: 978-1-952526-16-9

Credits

From *100 Flowers and How They Got Their Names* by Diana Wells and Ippy Patterson, copyright © 1997. Reprinted by permission of Algonquin Books, an imprint of Hachette Book Group, Inc.

Cover design by Water's Edge Press
Images licensed through iStock.com

A Water's Edge Press First Edition

Also by Joan Wiese Johannes

Mother Less Child, 2000
Myopic Nerve, 2005
Sensible Shoes, Alabama State Poetry Society, 2009
Happily Ever After, 2012
He Thought the Periodic Table Was a Portrait of God,
    Finishing Line Press, 2013

For Jeffrey

Acknowledgements

The author is grateful to the editors of the following publications in which these poems first appeared, some in different form:

Lamenting My Failure to Learn How to Tap Dance in **Allegro & Adagio Dance Anthology**; *Child-free* in **Revise the Psalm: Work Celebrating the Writing of Gwendolyn Brooks**; *Life Expectancy* in **1842 Review**; *Good Company, Whatever Comes Next, A Widow on the Empire Builder Looks Out the Window All the Way Through North Dakota,* and *No More Sunday* in **Third Wednesday**; *Charismatic Megafauna* and *The Skeletons in My Closet* in **California Quarterly**; *Why I Haven't Written* in **Stoneboat Literary Journal**; *From My Dream Journal, Disarmament,* and *Perhaps I Should* in **Ariel Anthologies**; *Lemons, Why I Exchanged the Angel You Sent Me, Painting the World Blue, Mantra with Sound Effects,* and *Blackest Humor* in **Fox Cry Review**; *Ruling the Veldt* and *Lullaby* in **Main Street Rag**; *In Witness Protection, History Lesson, Newborns Cry but Do Not Weep, Man Talking on His Cell Phone in the Airport, Their First Day of the Dead, Bad Days at Black Rock, Daydream in the Restaurant Washroom, Keep Out of Reach of Children and Pets,* and *Study Guide for Your Final Exam* in **Portage Magazine**; *Do Not Disturb* and *Hand-Me-Downs* in **Hummingbird**; *During the Sermon, The Skeletons in Your Closet, Pep Talk for Rubber Bands, Push Back,* and *Root Growth* on the **YourDaily Poem** website; *Root Growth* in **2020 LOCKDOWN**; *Hereditary Risk, Wish You Were Here,* and *Chocolate Decadence With Vanilla Icing* in **Verse Wisconsin**; *Hereditary Risk* in **The Burden of Light Anthology**; *This Love, Fragments of History, I Remember, The Snow Was Deeper Then, Every Spring,* and *Petiole* in **Wisconsin Poets' Calendars**; *This Love* in **Celestial Musings: Poems Inspired by the Night Sky**; *Fact About a Flower* and *There's a Party Upstairs* on **Skinnypoems** website; *Correspondence Concerning the Flowers* and *Note Posted Under the Lost Pet Notices* in **Free Verse**; *Don't Believe a Word I Say, New Year's Resolve, Massaging Her Husband's Mistress, A Journey Through the National Museum of African American History and Culture, NASA'S Mars Rover Dead After 15 Years* (Rover, original title), *A Whack Upside the Head, His Name was Sisyphus, You Tell Me Your Secrets,* and *The West is No Place for a Lady* in **Moss Piglet**; *Push Back* and *Are You Listening* in **Red Cedar Review**; *When I Becomes We* in **Pink Panther**; *In the Uncanny Valley* and *Garden of Stars* in **Star*Line**; *Wolf Spirit Speaks* in **A Time for Singing** and **Perspectives**; *A Blooming Scandal* on the **Rondeau Roundup** blog; *Mantra with Sound Effects* in the theatrical production created by Raeleen McMillion for **Renaissance Theatreworks**; *Abecedarian for Jazz* in **Peninsula Pulse**; *Integral Obscenities* in **Off Channel**; *My Dearest Nicholas* in **Letters in the Attic** broadside; *Stood Up at the Sheboygan County Fair, Robin's Egg, She's Never Known Their Names, Waking from Anesthesia, You Go, Girl, Writing a Poem About Ukraine, Fundamentals of Acting,* and *Why We Took Away Mom's Car Keys* in **Bramble**; *On Your 95th Birthday You Tell Me,* **Wisconsin Fellowship of Poets' website**; *I Have Forgiven My Cat, Perhaps,* and *Makes or Breaks* in **Verse Virtual**.

My Missteps

Lamenting My Failure to Learn How to Tap Dance 1
Push Back 2
During the Sermon 3
I Remember 4
The Snow Was Deeper Then 5
No More Sunday 6
Integral Obscenities 8
From My Dream Journal 9
There's a Party Upstairs 10
This Love 11
Why I Haven't Written 12
Hereditary Risk 14
The Elephant 15
Do Not Disturb 16
Lemons 17
Daydream in a Restaurant Washroom 18
Why I Exchanged the Angel You Sent Me 19
Good Company 20
Having Its Way With Me 21
The Petiole 22
I Have Forgiven My Cat, Perhaps 23
Wish You Were Here 24
Are You Listening? 26
Disarmament 27

Your Missteps

The Skeletons in Your Closet 31
Note Posted Under the Lost Pet Notices 32
Pep Talk for Rubber Bands 33
Blackest Humor 34
His Name Was Sisyphus 35
Why We Took Away Your Mother's Car Keys 36
Man Talking on His Cell Phone in the Airport 37
Study Guide for Your Final Exam 38
Abecedarian for Jazz 40

Double Abecedarian of New Year's Resolve 41
You Go, Girl 42
Dating Advice From Your Mother 44
Waking From Anesthesia 45
You Tell Me Your Secrets 46
On Your 95th Birthday, You Tell Me 48
Robin's Egg 49
The West is No Place for a Lady 50

Their Missteps

A Widow on The Empire Builder 55
She's Never Known Their Names 56
Fact About a Flower 57
Newborns Cry but Do Not Weep 58
Stood Up at the Sheboygan County Fair 59
Whatever Comes Next 60
Ruling the Veldt 61
In Witness Protection 62
Massaging Her Husband's Mistress 63
Lullaby 64
History Lesson 65
Their First Day of the Dead 66
A Journey Through the National Museum 67
Wolf Spirit Speaks 68
Garden of Stars 69
In the Uncanny Valley 70
Don't Believe a Word I Say 71
Keep Out of Reach of Children and Pets 72
A Blooming Scandal 73
Correspondence Concerning the Flowers 74
My Dearest Nicholas 76
Bad Days at Black Rock 77
Chocolate Decadence with Vanilla Icing 79

On the Right Foot

Child-free 83
When I Becomes We 84
Writing a Poem About Ukraine 85
NASA'S Mars Rover Dead After 15 Years 86
Life Expectancy 87
Every Spring 88
Cruel and Fair 89
Charismatic Megafauna 90
Root Growth 91
Fragments of History 92
A Whack Upside the Head 93
Mantra with Sound Effects 94
Fundamentals of Acting 95
Makes or Breaks 96
Perhaps I Should 97
Hand-Me-Downs 98
I Will Walk in Winter 99

MY MISSTEPS

Lamenting My Failure to Learn How to Tap Dance

Ain't got no
brush step paradiddle
double back essences,
spank step smack between
a pair of cross behinds.
No red-sequined spandex
black satin hottie pants
jump click,   slide-click-slide
No step-step   ball change glide!

(faster)

No
brush step paradiddle
double back essences,
spank step smack between
a pair of cross behinds.
No red-sequined spandex
black satin hottie pants
jump click,   slide-click-slide
No step-step ball change glide!

Push Back

Melons have seeds, phones have cords
nickels have buffalo heads
pizza comes in a Chef Boyardee box

I catch measles from my brother
give him mumps
get tonsillitis like my sister
the baby has pinworms

We play statue maker, kick the can
star light moon bright
red rover, red rover, let Joanie come over
Ollie ollie oxen free

Dad wears a white shirt
Mom wears a pleated skirt
I wear a midriff with pedal pushers
My Betsy McCall doll goes everywhere
in her wedding gown

Comics at the Five and Dime
Penny candy: jawbreakers, red wax lips
licorice whips, sputnik gum
A rabbit's foot for luck

Oh, what a colorful world
on black and white TV
Rin Tin Tin, Sky King, Howdy Doody
Summer-Fall-Winter-Spring

I ride my fat-tired bike
When the pedal is up, I push back
drag my other foot along the street
Stop time

During the Sermon

    for Beth

Perched in the choir loft,
our fathers watch us like hawks,
their mouths drawn
into thin, straight lines.

I pass you a gumdrop
and shift my gaze to read
the note you have written
on your bulletin.

In the front pew,
two foxes on the shoulders
of a blue-haired lady
bite down harder on their toes.

I Remember

I remember the drowned boy
leaving a wet shape on the dock,
my knees shaking bone on bone,
red ruffles on my swimsuit shivering,

leaving a wet shape on the dock.
I remember the red light quivering,
red ruffles on my swimsuit shivering,
my fingers clutching my cold arms.

I remember the red light quivering,
my teeth rattling,
my fingers clutching my cold arms
as the ambulance pulled away.

My teeth rattling,
my mother wrapping me in a towel
as the ambulance pulled away.
I remember the silence,

my mother wrapping me in a towel,
my knees shaking bone on bone.
I remember the silence.
I remember the drowned boy.

The Snow Was Deeper Then

The snow was deeper then.
It fell faster, drifted higher,
lasted longer into spring.

I survived winter wrapped
in scratchy wool that smelled
like old dogs and never dried
on the pegs in the hall.

Face hidden by a scarf, wet
with snot and condensation,
I dropped my outlaw guise
just long enough to steal
a breath of icy air

that chapped my cheeks
as rough and red as the rings
around my legs where
fake fur on leaky boots
rubbed my bare calves raw.

The snow was deeper then.
It fell faster, drifted higher,
lasted longer into spring.

No More Sunday

Drives in our two-tone Olds, counting horses,
holding up the ceiling and lifting our feet
when we passed a cemetery.
We yelled "Spud" when we saw a VW bug,
sang all those songs everybody knew
and begged Dad to drive faster at the crest
of each hill so we could fly.

My baby sister slept in Mom's arms,
my big sister read a book, and my brother and I
punched each other unrestrained in the back seat
until Dad threatened, "If I have to stop this car"—
then stopped the car,
not to spank our deserving butts, but because
our drive had brought us close to family or friends—
no invitation, no phone call, just
"We were out for a drive."

And Aunt Wanda, Uncle Roy, Edith and Louie,
or the Wilsons welcomed us into their home
still wearing the clothes they had worn to church,
their chicken dinners eaten, dishes washed,
and with nothing they would rather do
than jabber away the rest of the day,
and of course, have us stay for supper.

They had children or dogs for us to play with,
and the Braves or Cubs were playing, so the men
could talk with one ear tuned to the transistor radio
while the women visited, keeping an eye on us
and setting the table so we could share summer
sausage, cheese, homemade bread, whole milk;
and for the grown ups, coffee boiled on the stove.
After supper, we children were excused,
and Mom asked if we needed to use the bathroom.

She never believed me when I said I didn't have to,
but herded us to the car while Dad
and Louie or Uncle Roy or Mr Wilson
laughed at a joke we didn't get to hear.
Finally, they meandered down the driveway,
and Dad leaned against the bumper smoking
a Marlboro while Mom and Edith or Aunt Wanda
or Mrs. Wilson talked through the open window.

By the time we pulled out onto the road,
waved goodbye, and headed toward home,
the water tower was glowing in the setting sun,
my baby sister was asleep, the Burma Shave
          Slow down, Pa
          Sakes alive
          Ma missed signs
          Four
          And five
was fading into dusk, and I was wishing I had
gone to the bathroom when I had the chance.

Integral Obscenities

From the moment I wriggled out of the white gauze
womb and stripped every leaf from my natal tree,
I knew I was the nuisance all tent worms are.

That is why, by age fourteen,
I was ready to be born again as a snake.
Snakes have integral obscenities in their tales

of temptation, elation, salvation, damnation.
Adolescence is the acknowledgement of your inner snake.
Ask Freud or ask my Catholic friends, as new to me then

as pubic hair, budding breasts, that secret time of month.
They taught me Catholic as only young teens can,
not the You're-going-to-hell;-I-can't-play-with-you simplicity

of my childhood neighbor or the
They-crucify-Christ-while-we-praise-resurrection
propaganda of my protestant confirmation,

but the How-much- and- what- to-confess confusion
of pre-weight-of-the-world sin.
Is confessing five counts of not honoring your parents

instead of twenty-five a lie or just bad bookkeeping?
And how many times did I take the Lord's name in vain?
God, I was glad I only had to stop thinking

about inevitability and impossibility and sex
long enough to eat my crouton, drink my grape juice,
and promise not to sin again.

From My Dream Journal

In the dream I want to ask my father
what it feels like to take your last breath.

Is there an element of surprise
when inhale does not follow exhale,

a conscious realization that the breath
you have just released is your last?

But even in a dream, I know it is rude
to remind my father that he is dead,

so I dance around the question
and ask if being a mortician gave him

insight into what it's like to die.
I can tell he knows what I really want

to know, and while he thinks about how
much he is willing to tell me,

my newly-widowed friend at the edge
of my view walks briskly out of the room.

There's a Party Upstairs

"There's a Party Upstairs"
  dying
  New
  Year's
  Eve
  dying
  Dad
  dreams
  celebration
  dying
"There's a party upstairs"

This Love

Tonight the sky holds me
as if I am an errant star
in the jewel box of silence,
and I think of my father
and the shining absolutes
that ruled him.

Responsibility incarnate,
he set his feet,
fastened his belt,
and anchored in Orion;
I blazed and fell
in a shower of stars.

I feel him with me now
while stars cling to the sky
bracing themselves
for another night.
If he left me anything,
it was this love.

Why I Haven't Written

The fruit truck was in town yesterday,
and the tangelos are juicy and sweet;
the grapefruit are good too,
but for some reason my favorite coffee
doesn't taste as good as it used to.
This morning I saw a hawk on my walk
and finished embroidering the hotdog on
the towel with the restaurant motif, but I don't
have any tan floss so can't start on the bun.
So you can see my life is not worth the price
of a stamp; still I can't stop thinking about how
Dad wrote weekly even when he had no news.
He called those letters *nothing letters*,
but they were always about something;
I know I read them all, and when I visited him
on Saturdays, he always stopped at his mailbox
after lunch and usually had letters from each of us.
No matter how busy or boring our lives,
if we hadn't posted by Thursday,
those little angels on our shoulders put pens
in our hands and licked our stamps.
It made it easier to leave, knowing Dad
had letters to open, especially because his voice
always caught when he said, "Come back soon,"
which made my heart ache.
You know what I mean; we are all so alike.
Can it really be twelve years since Dad died?
Yes, I guess it can, so I should write and tell you
that the fruit truck was in town yesterday,
and the tangelos are juicy and sweet,
and the grapefruit are good too,
but for some reason my favorite coffee
doesn't taste as good as it used to,

and this morning I saw a hawk on my walk
and finished embroidering the hotdog
on the towel with the restaurant motif, but I don't
have any tan floss so can't start on the bun.
And I should add that I am grateful
that this is a nothing letter and I have no news.

Hereditary Risk

During colonoscopy
when I am not awake
but not asleep,
I dream
I turn over my feather bed
and find your bathrobe
pressed like a blue leaf
between pages of a book.

I am afraid of dreams
of you
and of the doctor
who may see in me
your shadow.

When you died, I changed
my food,
my weight,
my laugh,
my shoes;
everything that felt like you.

But umbilical cords
aren't really cut.
You are still
rounding out with me inside,
keeping me safe
or marking my cells
to self destruct.

Your bathrobe hangs
in my guest room.
Sometimes
when I miss you,
I put it on.

The Elephant

An elephant is standing in Mom's room.
Its great, gray presence casts a mournful pall.
I cannot speak of love or life or tomb.

Balloons and flowers fail to lift the gloom.
The monitor of vital signs shows all.
An elephant is standing in her room.

Mom is a rosebush in its final bloom.
I am an ugly, parasitic gall.
I cannot speak of love or life or tomb.

I long for comfort back inside her womb
cocooned within the birthing shroud of caul.
An elephant is standing in Mom's room.

We share the knowledge of forthcoming doom
without important words; our talk is small.
I cannot speak of love or life or tomb.

The predator of grief wants to consume
me, so I hide behind this silent wall.
An elephant is standing in Mom's room.
I cannot speak of love or life— or tomb.

Do Not Disturb

My calico cat lies dying
on my favorite sweater
drying on its rack by the sink

Lemons

I was squeezing lemons in the P.T.A.
food stand before the 4th of July parade
when I thought I saw you in the crowd
walking to the beat of incessant drums.
I put another sun-ball into the juicer,
pulled the lever,
then picked up another lemon
and did it again.
The woman beside me was scooping ice
into red, white, and blue cups
and boring me with too much
information about every sorry excuse
for a man she had ever known.
You know how some people
stop talking if you don't reply or nod?
Well, she wasn't one of them.
So, as horses bridled against bridles
and clowns squeezed into tiny cars,
I just kept silently murdering fruit,
having nothing to say about you.

Daydream in a Restaurant Washroom

When the shooting starts,
my guardian angel will try to pull me up
onto a toilet beside her, but I have seen
enough adventure films to know
the shooter is going to push on the stall door,
and when he
(yes, the shooter is going to be male)
finds it locked, he will shoot through it.
So, I will push my angel ahead of me
behind the door between us and the shooter,
and when the shooting stops
and approaching footsteps warn me
that I am about to fight for my life,
I will raise the plunger grabbed from this stall,
whack the gun out of his hands,
and smack him full in the face
with a left-hand-dominant swing like the one
that took out Andy Arneson's teeth when we
played softball in fourth grade phy ed.
Then I will grab the gun and hold him
at gunpoint until the police arrive,
which should be soon, since everyone
(except me)
has a cellphone and concealed weapon.
Finally, in the few safe seconds I have left,
I will glance at my guardian angel and see
a Mona Lisa smile on her alabaster face.
I will want to have faith in her, want to believe,
but I won't be able to trust her with my life.
She may be bulletproof, but I am not.

Why I Exchanged the Angel You Sent Me

   A Thank You Note I Didn't Send

I have never liked angels, especially cherubs,
who could be pre-born but look like dead babies to me.
This is disturbing, although not as disturbing
as the bimbo you sent me swaddled in white tissue
and nestled in a box tied with a gold elastic band.

I know I can't expect you to know everything,
and you were right that I am a spiritual person,
but this creature is your dream of a heavenly being—
not mine: bowling ball breasts, parted lips,
golden hair curling around alabaster cheeks,
and those ridiculous wings.

Angels don't need wings,
and they should look as if they know higher truths,
not as if they want to be carnally known by you.
Teddy bears can look as if they are trying
to know whatever it is they are supposed to know,
so you would have done better buying me a bear;
I would have kept and even liked it.

But I have just plopped *Gabriella* onto the counter
next to the Godiva chocolates
and will take several boxes of them home instead.
Those heavenly beings, who wrap their glorious
nakedness in gold foil, don't pretend at virtue,
openly invite me to eat their forbidden fruit.

Good Company

Every evening I hear the voices
no matter what I prepare,
but when I cook elegant meals
and set the table with fine china,
I hear praise for the marbling of beef
and the plumpness of poultry,
or warnings that calamari turns
into rubber bands if you forget
to carefully watch the time.

I am careful
about watching the time.

Sometimes I hear every word,
but usually the voices are like that
ringing that my doctor says is
one of those things that happen
as we age like forgetting
where we put our keys

or seeing dead people,
which happens

only now and then, and only
in glimpses when the sun
is setting and the angle of light
is just right so beams stream
through the sheer curtains
on my dining room window.

When that happens, it helps me
know how many places to set.

Having Its Way With Me

Now that I have little time
I get more done
and when I'm done
sleep comes
or if sleep does not come
I count the sheep of regret
and regret the murmuration
of lies and murmur
of half truths that mean
truth no longer matters
in a world in which
matter is transformed.
Clothing comes apart
at the seams
morphs into fabric
unravels into thread
rewinds itself on spools
only to be unwound
warped onto looms
woven into fabric
sewn into clothes
that come apart
at the seams
unraveling into thread.
In glaze of almost-sleep
I watch the Fates
spin and gauge
can't see the one who cuts
who is the source
of this discourse
the reason no reason
is my state of mind
and why in this state
I have little time
and time is having its way

The Petiole

Trees don't drop their leaves; leaves let go,
not with the plum-bob plunge of acorns
rat-a-tat-tatting against the bottom
of an aluminum boat,
but with the silent float of the man
who breezed past me to the cliff and stepped
into nothingness and all to drift
between mountains.
His red and yellow parasail spread
in cloudless sky, while I stood firm
in my belief that I would be crushed
against the crags if I ever tried to fly,
which is the reason I disregard the fall
of gold and scarlet leaves,
but hold in high regard that small apparatus,
like the mouth of a praying mantis,
that secures each leaf to its branch.

I Have Forgiven My Cat, Perhaps

I have forgiven my cat
for killing the finch
that escaped from its cage

perhaps
because there are no feathers
on the floor and because

even though there is no way
out of my living
room, I can tell myself

it flew away.
Or perhaps
I have forgiven my cat

because the finch
was a nameless bird,
and she is my Whiskers.

I have watched her
juggle filberts
dive into rumpled rugs
clutch pillows

in her claws and teeth,
tail twitching
with a life of its own.

She is always practicing
the kill
an essential skill

for those of us
who know
all games end the same.

Wish You Were Here

I would like to tell you
that we pass the time on the bus
discussing Tibetan sky funerals
and the one-child policy,
but the truth is we talk a lot
about what does or does not
come out of our bodies.
On any given day,
most of us have diarrhea,
some are constipated, and one
(who must have bribed the Buddha)
feels fine. We commiserate
about squatting over troughs
and porcelain holes in floors,
clutching the bottoms of doors
(if there are doors).
When I had heat stroke,
I didn't know if I should throw up
before or after squatting.
I don't wear a belt anymore
(takes too much time);
not splashing is everything.
We are running out of toilet paper
and sanitizer, pay to use facilities
you couldn't pay us to use back home,
and have developed an odd intimacy;
one guy admitted
to having the runs in his sleep
(panty-liners - not just for ladies anymore,
and how much do you tip the maid)?
We eat rice porridge for breakfast,
rice soup for lunch, rice for dinner;
and a celestial burial
sounds like Heaven right now.

After the monk cuts me into pieces,
vultures will carry me skyward.
These vultures are gigantic
and not as ugly as ours.
I am impressed.

Are You Listening?

In the dingy bar down the street
from our hotel, the patrons speak Italian,
but the infomercial projected on a sheet
tacked to the wall blares in English,
repeating its message about
The Earwax Removal System.
First, the device fills the screen.
Then a diagram of a clogged ear canal
dissolves into a close-up of a man
wincing as he shoves a Q-tip
too far into his ear. He yells, "Ouch!"
as the film cuts to a smiling woman
using the device to suck
wax out of her happy child's ear.
Then The Earwax Removal System
reappears, its 39-euro price tag
haloed in a star.

My Italian is limited to ordering wine
and buying *dua bigletti* for the vaporetto
so both of us had tickets to ride the canals
from San Marco's Cathedral to Gallerie
dell' Accademia to Scuolo San Rocco
so we could look at beheaded
and disemboweled saints all day,
but I know conversion rates well
enough to know that 39 euros is almost
55 dollars and that, although a gondola
ride costs 80 euros without musicians,
if we go now when the honeymooners
are renting them, we can listen to their music
without paying for our own.
The tour books say Venice is magic at night,
and tonight is our last chance.

Disarmament

Arced as an electrical current or adz,
beastly and bright, I burn, flay,
cut, and cull. I am a lethal ax
deflecting each dark arrow,
eluding enemies, sharp as a shiv.
Fiercely the club of Vishnu
guarantees not flight but fight,
harbors the vessel in which the lotus
in my heart grows on a spear.
Joined like the skins of an umiaq,
knit like chain mail, I wrap
lithe fingers around a stiletto,
malevolence fueling me, and then—

"No!" I softly say to the venom
oozing through me. I am an opal,
phoenix reborn, a light, and a lark.
Quietude enfolds me; Svaraj
reasserts herself. Joined, we are magi,
seventh rays of the sun, each breath
transcendent, a ritual blessing
urging me to trust my gentler self.
Violet as a trillium past prime,
wilted and by age diminished,
xeric as a mirage of rainbow arc
yearning for rain, I want to climb,
zenith nearing, armed only with aura.

Your Missteps

The Skeletons in Your Closet

Every time you leave the house,
the skeletons in your closet
dress up in your clothes.
The oldest zips too-tight silk
capris over her fleshless thighs
and slides her metatarsals
into stiletto heels.
The youngest dips phalanges
into the pockets
of your vintage blazer.
Its padded shoulders define
her clothes hanger frame
as she executes a run-way turn.
The skeleton you want to forget
slips into the satin night gown
that sinks into her pelvic bowl.
The rest of them stand restlessly
waiting to cover wild bones
with the coyote jacket
you have never worn.
They like to pretend
they are hunting rabbits,
snapping their yellow teeth,
and laughing at themselves
and at these clothes that remind
them of what they are
and remind you of who you were.

Note Posted Under the Lost Pet Notices

You probably don't remember me, but I am wondering
why you no longer do your laundry on Friday nights.
You are the guy in your thirties who wore nice shirts,
usually plaid, suggesting that you came here from work,
which is good because I like men who work.

Your shirts were wrinkled, so I figured you were single.
And since you didn't wash your sheets every week,
I surmised that you weren't getting a lot, which is good
because a girl can't be too careful these days.

Your underwear impressed me; briefs are unpretentious,
and you replace them before they go gray or the elastic dies.
I also liked the way you rolled your socks into little balls
before tossing them into your bag. You never missed,
which is good because I like men who are athletic.

I didn't speak to you the first time I saw you because
I was wearing old, green sweatpants.
The next week, not expecting to see you again,
I wore my glasses and my hair was dirty.
Once I introduced you to *Bounce* when your towel stuck
to your tee shirt but was too shy to introduce myself.

Now I miss our meetings and hope you have just changed
your laundry schedule and haven't lost your job, moved,
or found someone to iron your shirts.

Pep Talk for Rubber Bands

Tangled in this junk drawer
like a mass of mating snakes,
remember that you are versatile.

You seal bags of goldfish at county fairs,
prevent candles from wobbling,
clasp newspapers so they'll hit the porch,
hold asparagus in orderly bundles.

You are flexible enough to
power wind-up toys,
twist into kitschy bracelets,
tolerate the stretch and snap of fidgeters,
torment teachers' pets.

You are strong enough to
stabilize needles in tattoo guns,
snap the wrists of habitual nail biters,
secure masks on people's faces,
stop toddlers from opening cabinet doors.

Take heart— you have potential;
you are the connective force giving braces
the power to straighten human teeth.

Blackest Humor

You aim your finger like a pistol
against the side of your head
and pull an imaginary trigger
when she recites again
the litany of aunts and uncles,
their faults, and how they died.
Click
Bang
You are so dead
I keep count each time
I hear the story of her dog Tarzan
who swallowed poison
and died such a horrible death;
your sister has promised
to buy me a shot of good gin
every time Tarzan dies.
Splash
Glug
I am so drunk

We fear and loathe your mother
's dementia,
fear and loathe the people
we've become
Click
Bang
We are so dead
Splash
Glug
We are so drunk
Ya Ya
We are so dead
drunk

His Name Was Sisyphus

Dementia is your mother hiding
her hearing aids and stuffing tissues
into her pockets until they bulge
like hamsters' cheeks.
I have emptied every pocket
in every pair of slacks in her closet,
and as the mountain of Kleenex grows
in the middle of her bed, I ask myself
if this is my life now, searching
for hearing aids day after day.
Your mother looks confused as I
unfold each tissue as if she has no idea
how those tissues got into her pockets
because she has no idea how
those tissues got into her pockets,
but I am afraid I will throw out
a hearing aid if I am less than
diligent in my searching.
Then I look under pillows and cushions,
in pillow cases and between sheets,
in sewing boxes, covered dishes,
cupboards and dresser drawers.
I find jewelry, knitting needles,
dog collars and leashes; she thinks
her dog can't be stolen without a leash.
Finally, between a three-year-old
Readers' Digest and a knitting magazine
with a baby in a blue sweater on the cover,
I find a hearing aid.
I am giddy with joy— for a moment.
Then I remember that Greek guy
(What was his name?)
who pushed that stone
up the hill, up the hill, up the hill.

Why We Took Away Your Mother's Car Keys

The sun is setting when your mom arrives.
She tells me semis blew past her
and a white limousine rode her bumper
until she saw a sign for Eden
and took the exit.
The old road lined with gold-
leafed trees was gone.
The new road went past Walmart.
When she saw a green dinosaur,
she turned at the Sinclair station
and headed home.
But Eden is south of Oshkosh,
and Mom has no reason to go there.
I ask where she was going,
and she looks at me as if I should know,

just looks at me as if I should know
when I ask where she was going,
since your mom has no reason to go
to Eden, south of Oshkosh.
And headed home,
she turns at the Sinclair station
when she sees a green dinosaur.
The new road goes past Walmart.
Leafed trees lie ahead—
the old road lined with gold.
And she takes the exit
when she sees a sign for Eden.
A white limousine pulls over;
no semis blow past her.
The sun is setting when your mom arrives.

Man Talking on His Cell Phone in the Airport

When your kids come home with perfect attendance
be proud of that stuff,
every little thing.
Keep that stuff.
Don't throw it in the trash.
Education— Mama couldn't pay for it.
I got a scholarship.
You can take everything else,
but you can't take that degree from me.
That is why I put my diploma on the wall.
I got out of jail on Monday.
You know what I'm saying, Brother?

You know what I'm saying, Bro.
I got out of jail on Monday.
That is why I put my diploma on the wall.
You can't take that degree from me,
but you can take everything else.
I got a scholarship.
Education— Mama couldn't pay for it.
Don't throw it in the trash.
Keep that stuff,
every little thing.
Be proud of that stuff
when your kids come home with perfect attendance.

Study Guide for Your Final Exam

I. True or False

Answers both answer and produce more questions,
more statements are true than false,
but if part of a statement is false, it's false.
Never, only, or *always* statements are seldom true:
> Wise men always make wise choices.
> Only fools make the same mistakes twice.
> There can *never* be more than one love of your life.

Generally, sometimes, and *often* indicate truth:
> Slacking is sometimes beneficial to morale.
> Morale boosting is generally good.
> Good thinking often results in success.

Remember, white lies aren't really white;
they are like snow that falls through pristine air,
then is sprinkled with snow fleas
as soon as it touches the ground.

II. Multiple Choice

Usually wrong answers precede the right one:
A woman who marries more than once is
> A bride more than a bridesmaid
> Believes in marriage as a temporary state
> Can see a need for change
> Defines herself in someone new.

Choose C if you're not sure, but statistically
B is almost as likely; trust your intuition.
Remember, *None of the Above* and *All of the Above*
are seldom the answer, so even if you think
each leaf-coated sphere of unassembled snowman
> really looks like three huge meatballs,
> a trio of hedgehogs, your father's clay marbles,
> and the ghost of Christmas past,

choose the best answer.

III. Essay

Make sure you understand the question, budget your time,
and determine if your opinion matters
or if you must rely on facts. For facts, quote experts.
If your essay can be personal, tell your readers
that each winter your husband and you lie down
and wave your arms and legs until angels appear.
Detail is important;
say you have pledged to do this yearly until
the rescue squad has to pull you out of the snow.
If you have time left, proofread your work.
Neater papers usually receive higher scores.

Abecedarian for Jazz

A symphony is formal, unlike jazz.
Black-tied and tailed, musicians play
collectively a measured score: complex,
defined, composed in high-brow
elegance— But jazz can rev
flat hearts like déjà vu,
grabbing us with no restraint,
hurling us into a world of no constraints
imposed by rules— Let improv roar,
jazz being everything but tranq,
kick-ass splendid, a wild ruckus romp!
Like inhibitions joyfully let go,
mad music bops with jubilation when
New Orleans musicians meet to jam.
Oh, when pulse and cadence call
percussively, and wild timbres clank,
quicken as this not-so-sacred haj
refolds your soul in origami
shaped into an angel flying high
toward the heaven of parlando song.
Unlimited by meter, oblivious to clef,
vital, charged and feeling so alive,
wake up with spirit sensitized,
xanthene-dyed fluorescent while the maniac
you have become now jazzed and numb
zings into a syncopated tra— la la!

Double Abecedarian of New Year's Resolve

Any other day, I'd play your wild jazz,
but today, not precisely knowing why,
classic calm, and not your sensual sax,
delights me with fresh longing for new
endeavors, inspires me to freely improv;
forget the keys, notes, and melodies you
gladly play because it is now time to start
harkening to my music, living my songs.
I have been far too long a slave to master,
joined to you, not saying *talaq, talaq, talaq;**
quiet, unheard, off-stage, no mic, no amp;
longing for, but not reaching for, the solo
magic of giving life to music of my own.
Now driven by a new year's momentum,
opportunity appears like a precious jewel
plundered from a crown for me to pluck
quite easily, with no help from king or raj.
Ripe with desire, I reach out for the life I
should have lived before. Even though
time was wasted, it is my friend, jamming
upbeat, undying, eager to take in my riff,
vibrant as it is, filled with fresh exuberance
without the once-felt shyness, fear, or dread.
X, that unknown, lurks, but I am euphoric,
yearning to step out on that proverbial limb,
zip-line aimed toward anywhere— Ta da!

*Traditional Islamic law gave the husband the right
to divorce his wife using this announcement.

You Go, Girl

If you let a knife fall into dishwater,
it stabs you, so caution has been key
to your survival in this oppressive, pedal
to the metal existence with its cat
of nine tails lashing at you, and the rib-
aching rejection from his yacht club set.

You passively watch as concrete sets
over your escape hatch, while dishwater
gray, the keel breaks away from the ribs
of your lifeboat, your rescue car's key
snaps in the ignition, the hydraulic cat
stalls in the sand, your bike loses its pedal.

Experience has taught you to soft-pedal
your way around your husband, to set
your sights low; and like a scaredy cat,
glide silently through the dishwater
and toilet bowl cleaner world that key-
note your sorry life as Adam's rib.

He bullies, belittles, and ribs
you, pushes you down like the pedal
on his shiny new car. The keys
to his heart are his corvette and set
of golf clubs. You are just dishwater
headed for the drain, a drowning cat.

But with lives to spare, a clever cat
can architect its life, and you could rib
an arch to walk through, dishwater
days done, while like piano pedals
pulsing through a grammy-winning set,
you modulate your life into a major key.

It is long past time for you to key-
punch your own card, sit in the cat-
bird seat, transform into a vintage set
of china on which to serve prime rib.
Play the giant's golden harp with pedal
point sustained; bathe in rose, not dishwater.

Blonde that dishwater, neuter that cat,
steal the answer key, spare that extracted rib,
floor that pedal; win game, match, and set.

Dating Advice From Your Mother

Do not run from lightning.
Running gathers moisture around you
and KABOOM!
Lightning strikes randomly—
         the cross on the steeple,
         the chicken coop,
         the cow and her calf.
It starts buildings on fire and triggers the alarms.
One bolt killed forty sheep.
There are stories of carrots cooking in the ground.
Each bolt has several strokes, the last upward.
Electrocution occurs
when the current goes up one leg and down the other.
People have been stripped naked,
left unharmed.
Lightning can strike the same place twice.
Trust me.

Trust me.
Lightning can strike the same place twice.
Left unharmed,
people have been stripped naked.
When the current goes up one leg and down the other,
electrocution occurs.
Each bolt has several strokes, the last upward.
There are stories of carrots cooking in the ground.
One bolt killed forty sheep.
It starts buildings on fire and triggers the alarms.
         The cow and her calf,
         the chicken coop,
         the cross on the steeple—
lightning strikes randomly
and KABOOM!
Running gathers moisture around you.
Do not run from lightning.

Waking From Anesthesia

Waking from anesthesia is
a calendar page missing
so your birthday never comes,
a sleepwalk to Grandma's house,

a calendar page missing
while goblins carry off the little girl,
a sleepwalk to Grandma's house,
a skipping stone sinking

while goblins carry off the little girl.
"It is time to wake up," the nurse says.
A skipping stone sinking,
you struggle to swim.

"It is time to wake up," the nurse says.
Her voice is so far away
you struggle to swim
toward the blurry light.

Her voice is so far away
so your birthday never comes
toward the blurry light
waking from anesthesia is.

You Tell Me Your Secrets

My only childhood pet was a turtle
that lived longer than my grandpa.
Gramps had a voice like sandpaper
and always kept a patterned, red
bandana in his pocket and a light
for the cigarettes he smoked in secret.

After his stroke, smoking was *our* secret,
and after the salmonella scare, my turtle
was hidden in the basement under a light-
bulb hooked to the bench where Grandpa
had once repaired furniture with his red-
handled tools and multi-grade sandpaper.

I loved to listen to that raspy sandpaper
sound, its whispering music like a secret
being shared as Grandpa told me things red-
blooded boys should know while my turtle
basked in its plastic lagoon, and Grandpa
talked and smoked beneath the dingy light.

Usually our discourse was easy and light
as the shushing sound of sandpaper,
but occasionally he lost control, and Grandpa
let loose. Those times were also our secret
like his cigarettes and my contraband turtle.
I didn't tell Mom about the times he saw red.

That's because I knew his anger was a red
herring, a feeble way for him to make light
of the fact that he felt as helpless as a turtle
on its back, his heart worn thin as sandpaper,
cigarette smoking habit not really a secret,
his days fatefully numbered. Poor Grandpa!

I had no close friends except my Grandpa,
no baseball team, Boy Scout troop, *red
rover red rovering* neighbor kids, just secrets
with Gramps and pretending to be light-
hearted while, feeling roughly sandpapered,
I hid my thin skin in a shell like my turtle.

My childhood was secrets, a dying grandpa,
love for a pet turtle; and patterned, red
bandanas, dingy light, and sandpaper.

On Your 95th Birthday, You Tell Me

These days I sense the closing of the door
that through the years was always open wide.
My little boat waits tethered on the shore.

I do not have the strength to launch it nor
the will to even take a walk outside.
These days I sense the closing of the door.

The pleasures of my youth are now a chore;
why hike or row when you can rest or ride?
My little boat waits tethered on the shore.

Asleep, I dream that I am three or four,
a pre-teen, adolescent or a bride;
and yet, I sense the closing of the door.

Today I wish for less instead of more.
More than my share I've had; I'm satisfied.
My little boat waits tethered on the shore.

And mindful of what nature has in store,
I'm ready for what cannot be denied.
These days I sense the closing of the door;
my little boat waits tethered on the shore.

Robin's Egg

I have found you,
tiny blue cup,
in the grass outside my door,
and your presence assures me
that tomorrow brings gifts,
emptiness has substance,
and even though I never find
both halves of hatched egg,
I will not die alone.

Oh, bowl of blue mystery
that fits on my thumb,
helmet that shields me
from the falling of the sky,
halfness that is whole,
herald of a songster,
naked and new —
let me be satisfied with you,
with just your bit of blue.

The West is No Place for a Lady

Going out west can get in your blood
red as the real imitation cowgirl boots
your high-class mom won't buy her little miss.
It can pulse through your veins, dog
you like a pesky little sister, train
you to set your sights on settling the plains.

But it won't matter when you go; it's as plain
insane for present-day blue-bloods
to fly in planes as it was to join wagon trains
and go Westward Ho-ing out where a boot
in the butt waits for every pedigreed dog
that wanders west of The Big Miss.

This is the God-awful truth, so don't miss
my point: if you're Calamity Jane or just plain
Jane, there's no back door to the prairie dog
hole you're going to find yourself in, bloody
and beaten, dying with your pretty boots
on or off, moaning like the whistle of a train.

Out there, it's never been true that "This train
is bound for glory", and if you miss
your chance to get out of Dodge, it's Boot
Hill, sure as shooting. It doesn't get any plainer—
You'll be the center of the target, the blood
red bulls eye, the sun and not its shadow dog.

You aren't a match for those junkyard dogs,
and there just isn't any way to untrain
them, which means you won't find any blood
brothers there. So excuse me, sweet missy,
but I always tell the truth and speak plain,
and the west is going to give you the boot.

You'll never, like that clever Puss in Boots,
gain fame and fortune in that dog-eat-dog
terrain that pounds your kind into the plains
with the Indians and outlaws while the train
wreck that's coming is surely not going to miss
you. Believe me, the west is out for your blood.

Still off to the Plains? Get yourself some sturdy boots;
and remember salt takes out blood stains, Little Dogie,
and when you shoot from the train, don't miss.

THEIR MISSTEPS

A Widow on The Empire Builder Looks Out the Window All the Way Through North Dakota

On a day as gray as her hair,
sunflowers with heavy heads
look down at the ground
as far as she can see,

sunflowers with heavy heads
in fields flooded into marsh land.
As far as she can see,
hay bales sink in pools of water

in fields flooded into marsh land
and hawks always flying alone.
Hay bales sink in pools of water.
Another sweep of dark birds

and hawks always flying alone,
a small herd of grazing cattle,
another sweep of dark birds.
Cranes stand still as saplings.

A small herd of grazing cattle
look down at the ground.
Cranes stand still as saplings
on a day as gray as her hair.

She's Never Known Their Names

Margaret doesn't know their name,
so to her they are just little blue flowers
that bloom in May, delicate and soft
as the sweater her grandma wore
draped over her shoulders.
It was the color of her mother's eyes,
the only blue in a family of green,
not the glittery green of that
semi-precious stone, but the dark
jade of the little, carved turtle
on her sitting room shelf.
Margaret loves the yellow birds
that turn gray in winter
and the red bird that comes
to the feeder every day.
Red is her favorite color because
it is the color of those flowers
that look like flamenco dancers' skirts.
She likes purple too,
especially the shade of those blossoms
that perfume early summer nights
like the one on which she fell in love.
She thinks of him in summer
when the shiny leaves on those trees
that tremble in a breeze turn
their silvery sides to the sun;
she thinks of him also in winter
when withering leaves cling
to those trees that won't let go.

Fact About a Flower

Always twining clockwise
programmed
morning
glories
grow
programmed
like
some
people
programmed
always turning clockwise

Newborns Cry but Do Not Weep

The Chemistry of Tears

Tears are antibodies, enzymes, and salts
blended in the beaker of the brain,
but they also contain the water of life.
So why does she slice onions
to make tears flow, and why does she
catch them in little glass bottles
and place them on loved one's graves
when she knows spirits can tell
the difference between lacrimation
and the Prolactin-rich tears
that ease our pain.
She can't fool them, so she sets down
the knife, goes outside, crosses the yard,
climbs the fence into her neighbor's field
and approaches the buffalo
fattening for market.
She rests her hand on its head,
perhaps in invocation or at least
in something that feels like God.
She speaks the name she has given
the great beast and then tells it secrets
she can never tell a living or departed soul.
It shifts its weight, lightly stamps its foot,
and stares past her through eyes
that see clearly left and right,
but cannot focus on what is ahead.
She knows a scapegoat is a sacrifice,
not a victim,
and thinks that maybe after it is over,
she will be able to cry.

Stood Up at the Sheboygan County Fair

Crazy for being so lonely,
she pulls tufts of sweetness
from a cotton candy tutu
as big as Dolly Parton's hair
while the thickening August air
sticks the spun-pink cyclone
stiff as an Aquanet do.
She is pretending to watch
a juggler in a sequined vest
spin plates on poles, gliding
from one to the next,
tweaking them when they
wobble like alien spacecraft
falling from the sky, but she is
really eyeing the entrance,
ready to jump up and wave.

Suddenly a thunder
of raindrops
pounds the grandstand,
spit-waxes the stage,
and sends the juggler
slipping, sliding, and falling
through a waterfall
of fractured china plates.
He sputters to his feet,
falls again, and she
laughs until tears roll down
her cheeks and rosy goo
runs down her wrist,
leaving her holding
just a paper cone in her hand.

Whatever Comes Next

Lace curtains wave from the living room window.
In the window box, a red geranium blooms.

While she wrestled her trunk out the door,
the neighbor's cat crept in and now is purring

in the sunlight that streams through the window.
The taxi driver loads her sorry life into his cab.

By the time her husband gets home, clouds will have
hidden the sun, and the cat will be sprawled on the bed

exposing its soft belly to whatever comes next.
Fortunately, it has nine lives.

Ruling the Veldt

Some days sex is a tulip
redder than blood,
a challis of storm fronts
clashing—
hot air rushing into cold.

On those days contentment
counts for nothing;
her life becomes a glacier,
rigid as paralysis,
slow as a sloth.

Some days she reaches
for anything reckless,
sharp as a strip of tin—
shiny, forbidden,
tempting and light.

Then she feels ripe
for walking away from love,
lioness self-satisfied—
selfish, wild, and wise.

In Witness Protection

After another night
of country tunes and Coors

a leather-tanned creature
whose bottle-blonde hair
hangs like straw beneath

a star spangled bandana,
throws her aching leg
over Harley's
(his real name)
Harley,

bursitis reminding her
of that other woman
she wants us to forget.

Oh, say can you see
the woman she used to be?

Massaging Her Husband's Mistress

She sighs as I massage her temples
and slide my fingers across her forehead
until my strong thumbs

press against her eyelids
and feel the vulnerable orbs beneath.
I stroke the line of her jaw,

eager fingers on her slender throat.
I can feel her pulse
beat against my well-trained hands.

She doesn't know I know
as she lies on the scarlet towels
I have spread on my table just for her.

From the CD player, an Aeolian harp
moans its wind song, a rain stick rasps
its rattlesnake weave through sand.

Lullaby

Aunt Ruby sings her witching song,
enfolds us in a purple light
and the dark scent of plums.
My infant sister sleeps,
her fitful crying quelled
by melody and mode.
"Be careful," Mama pleads.
She can see through the veil,
and there is only a thread
between sleep and death.

Between sleep and death
there is only a thread
she can see through the veil.
"Be careful," Mama pleads.
By melody and mode,
her fitful crying quelled,
my infant sister sleeps,
and the dark scent of plums
enfolds us in a purple light.
Aunt Ruby sings her witching song.

History Lesson

My sister lies to her children.
When we see dozens of pig snouts
squeezing between slats of a truck bed,
she says the farmer is taking them on vacation.

When we see dozens of pig snouts
breathing their final breaths,
she says the farmer is taking them on vacation.
I picture them riding the Coney Island Cyclone

breathing their final breaths.
I don't want to think about the truth.
I picture them riding the Coney Island Cyclone.
Pigs are smarter than dogs, you know.

I don't want to think about the truth
squeezing between slats of a truck bed.
Pigs are smarter than dogs, you know.
My sister lies to her children.

Their First Day of the Dead

My nephew's blonde daughter beams for the camera
next to her kindergarten teacher, Señora Romero,
in front of La Calavera Catrina, Grande Dame of the Dead.
The skull-faced mariachi band strikes up a spirited tune.

Next to her kindergarten teacher, Señora Romero,
a dark-eyed child smiles from an etched-silver frame.
The skull-faced mariachi band strikes up a spirited tune
beside a plate of M&M's, a toy truck, and little sneakers.

A dark-eyed child smiles from an etched-silver frame.
The Virgin Mary is decoupaged on a tortilla
beside a plate of M&M's, a toy truck, and little sneakers
draped with a string of black onyx rosary beads.

The Virgin Mary is decoupaged on a tortilla.
A photo garland of 43 students kidnapped on their school bus
draped with a string of black onyx rosary beads
hangs above an altar decorated with sugar skulls.

A photo garland of 43 students kidnapped on their school bus
in front of La Calavera Catrina, Grande Dame of the Dead
hangs above an altar decorated with sugar skulls.
My nephew's blonde daughter beams for the camera.

A Journey Through the National Museum of African American History and Culture

A load of humankind in chains runs light,
so iron ballast bars were used to weight
the hold and keep the slaver's ship upright
when it set sail from Africa that day.

The captives tumbled in the toss and sway
of filthy hold, their homeland lost to sight.
When far at sea beyond the sheltered bay,
a load of humankind in chains runs light.

In darkness, bound together, shackles tight,
and stacked like wood, men on each other lay.
Each dawn exposed new casualties of night,
so iron ballast bars were used to weight.

When let on deck, men dared to disobey.
Still shackled, with no hope, they chose to fight
and hasten death, since living meant to stay
in the hold and keep the slaver's ship upright.

The women, raped and bruised, when given light
and air, jumped overboard; the only way
to live was drown and give the soul free flight
when it set sail for Africa that day.

The energy in shackles here displayed,
and power surge through iron now ignite
the flames of spirits from the past who pray
in pain and sorrow, haunting black and white—
a load of humankind in chains.

Wolf Spirit Speaks

He beat me with a branch of myrtle wood,
prepared to die before he'd lose a sheep.
That shepherd is the archetype of good.

Between his frightened flock and me he stood
among the stones, the hillside stark and steep.
He beat me with a branch of myrtle wood.

I doubt if any other shepherd would
have been as vigilant, not caught asleep.
That shepherd is the archetype of good.

He fought me to the death as shepherd should
and left my body in a battered heap.
He beat me with a branch of myrtle wood.

My death I understand and understood,
since as we sow, so also must we reap.
That shepherd is the archetype of good.

But his great purpose now misunderstood,
his flock has strayed, and only willows weep.
They'll hang him on a branch of myrtle wood,
that Shepherd who is archetype of Good.

Garden of Stars

She hadn't planned on living this long,
but that was nothing new;
she had never planned anything,
and it was entirely out of the blue
that she invited the robot gardener
to live in the planetarium her late husband
had installed in the cellar.
She never intended to spend so much
time down there gazing at stars and listening
to the gardener's steady voice calling
The Pleiades a cluster of honeysuckle
and telling her that meteor showers
were epidemics of leaf drop.
It did not have the language of astronomy,
but her garden had dried up long ago,
and the store of longevity pills
her husband had hoarded was infinite.
She had no reason to climb the stairs,
no reason to leave the garden of stars.
It was always midsummer night there,
and the robot called her his millennium rose.
Under his care she bloomed.

In the Uncanny Valley

Actuators raise my android arms, my
biomimetic body responds to my brain; if
conscience really is what makes us human,
do I dare trust mine or should you over-ride the
ethical adapter that enables me to choose, but
forces me to face frontiers with programmed
guilt? A gift, I guess if guilt, too, makes me
human. Still, the horror in your face
indicates that I am a mirror imperfect. "I'm
just a robot," I've been taught to say to
keep at bay your thoughts of killing me. You see,
like you, I want to live, but unlike you,
murder is not on my mind. My
network of neural fibers fears
oblivion, but won't obey the inner voice that tells me to
push you over the precipice, protect my not-
quite human self. I observe you as you
rationalize your rage, insist that I'm not real,
see silicone, and eye blinks nanoseconds slow as
technology tempts us in this treacherous terrain, this
Uncanny Valley, universe unknown. Here the
vicious nature of your nature is your vice. You
walk with weapon raised; your willing laser
X-marks the spot where my circuit will break.
Yea, though I walk no more, I reach toward you,
zombie-like hands entreating a-nn-ddd zzzzzzzzzz.

Don't Believe a Word I Say

A Survivor's Journal

A conga line of toads is dancing on the stove,
quiet as my cousin's laugh,
that silent wheeze that comes out her nose.
This amuses my Aunt June,
but she is from Oklahoma where amusement
follows people like a faithful dog.
Yesterday I carried fire in my hands
and washed my hair with the song of a wren.
I lied about the fire; I like to stick to the truth
when I can, especially now
that the thirsty Chicken of Death
wants to drink my blood.
It's thinner than the hormone-laced water
in her drinking dispenser cup
and probably tastier too.
Sometimes I sneak up behind that fowl
and kick her into a feather-flop
just so she doesn't forget that I resent
the way she gets away with murder
and am tired of trying to be inconspicuous
while she struts through the barnyard
parading her unpredictable certainty.
Her tomorrows are as pine-fresh as gin,
but mine just turn each day into a yesterday,
and the dead opossum rots a little more
beneath my porch.
Some reckonings happen slowly, you know,
but some are quick—
"Ouch! Ouch! Ouch!" cries the toad
at the end of the conga line.
The Chicken of Death just pecked out its eyes.

Keep Out of Reach of Children and Pets

The pharmacist fills her prescription and tells my golden retriever
that bad side effects my occur.
Sophie knows what "bad" means, so she looks down at the floor.
Then when he tells her not to drive, operate machines,
or sign contracts until she knows how the drug affects her,
she rests her head on her paws.

He warns that Ciprofloxacin may cause tendons to tear,
and I add that he means she can't play frisbee or chase rabbits.
He also says she might have trouble sleeping, nightmares
and hallucinations, or see or hear things that aren't there.
Sophie tilts her head and lifts one eye brow, so I remind her
of the way she bristles and growls at the dark patio door.

Then the pharmacist asks if she thinks she may be pregnant
or plans to get pregnant. I shake my head: not an issue.
Of course, she might still have to cope with diarrhea, wheezing,
difficulty talking, vaginal itching, and hives;
and she should avoid the sun because she will burn more easily.

Finally the pharmacist sternly warns her that there is a very bad
(Sophie closes her eyes) skin reaction called
Stevens-Johnson Syndrome toxic epidermal necrolysis
and repeats "very bad"!
(Sophie buries her nose in her paws
even before he says it may cause death).

I think Sophie has fallen asleep, but the pharmacist instructs
her to be sure to let him know if her heartbeat doesn't feel right,
she experiences thinking that isn't normal, lacks interest in life,
or has thoughts of killing herself.

A Blooming Scandal

Forget-me-nots grow in her pubic hair
the gossips say, and one man surely knows,
her gamekeeper who plants his seeds down there,
the man who calls her labia his rose.

Lord Chatterley must know, we all suppose
with all the talk about the trysting pair,
that hidden by his bored wife's underclothes,
forget-me-nots grow in her pubic hair.

Most women of her station would not dare
face condemnation that her class bestows,
but Lady Chatterley has not a care
the gossips say, and one man surely knows.

When not protecting pheasant chicks from crows
or catching pesky weasels in his snare,
he kisses Constance from her head to toes,
her gamekeeper who plants his seeds down there.

And though her reputation's past repair,
her carnal self is radiant and glows
thanks to her partner in this wild affair—
the man who calls her labia his rose.

Their scandal lives in poetry and prose,
so moralists and censors should beware,
since gossip spreads like fire, I propose
the thought that it will live as long as they're
forget-me-nots.

Correspondence Concerning the Flowers

The most memorable place they grew, however, was in Lady Chatterley's pubic hair, where her game keeper lover planted them, saying, "There's for-get-me-nots in the right place."

From *100 Flowers and How They Got Their Names*

My Dearest Sister,

I cannot begin to recount the chagrin I feel since hearing
of the flowers blooming in your private parts.
I have bravely born the shame you bring to our good name,
but the indelicacy of knowing you are continually moist
in that region of which I cannot speak and of which I loathe
myself for thinking for the time it takes to pen these words,
fills me with despair. In truth, I am not at all recovered
from my faint, and fear though smelling salts revive me here,
I may remain confined for quite a time, suffering as I do
from palpitations of the heart, which if I become alarmed,
attempt to thrust the organ through my modest breast.

Be that as it may, although I never thought I'd say
I thank the lord Dear Mother rests within her grave,
I am today most grateful, lest this revelation of your pubic
indiscretion send her there and make her rest unsweet.
Thus, the duty falls to me, unpleasant though it be, to beg
you attend to hygiene if, indeed, you must proceed
with this affair on which the local gossips feed so richly.
No doubt, your love, employed as lowly as he is, has grown
accustomed to the gaminess of fox and thus can do without
the niceties which gentlemen of breeding cannot forego,
but ladies need dip hankies in perfume when stench as vile
as the flatulence of lap-sized dogs assaults, which I surmise
must pale beside the odor of a body so untouched by
soap and watered in immoral ways to bring to blossom
scandalous blue blooms.

                                              Most truly,
                                              Your Loving Hilda

Dear Hilda,

Sorry to hear of your distress and to know that you
profess the cause of your ill health and deep despair
lies in the rumor of flowers growing in my pubic hair,
but though you are too dear for me to call you wrong,
I think that you should know that you are misinformed.
Our mother no more sweetly rests than you, having long
since molded in the tomb. I dare say she would grateful be
for a nosegay of forget-me-nots to freshen up her rot.
And since she made us in the usual way, upon her back
beneath our father's weight, I doubt that she would faint
to hear that I a woman am; in fact, she's grinning now
since worms have eaten through her rosy lips.

As for the need for hygiene, I agree; a lady whose spaniel
nuzzles in her lap assuredly must need a gross of soap
to keep her sweet, but though this come as a surprise,
there are better ways to cleanse your thighs.
I also take offense at your pretense of feminine concern
that I have found a love beneath myself and thus endure
a coupling coarser that the love a gentleman bestows.
Believe me, it is I who am beneath; a man who knows
his game does know his game, and play it well we do.
Perhaps it is the company you keep, those vile gossips
of whom you speak, that causes your heart to give you
so much pain. I think another organ thrust below your
modest bust would end your palpitations and
make you more robust.
                                    Love always,
                                    Lady C.

My Dearest Nicholas

I am awed by the way you saved my marriage
(and perhaps your life)
when my husband surprised you in our living room
last Christmas Eve.
Grabbing the cotton ball snow from my centerpiece
and my fur-trimmed red cape to disguise yourself
before Clement burst through the door was brilliant.
How cleverly you hid, under the tree,
the diamond bracelet you had brought for me;
and only someone with your athletic prowess
could have wriggled up the chimney far enough
to make my husband think you were gone.
You are a genius, my love, and my husband's inspiration
since the poem he wrote that night, although he deems it
beneath his dignity, was published and caused
a great sensation. By now you must have read it,
and I imagine your twinkling eyes are laughing at how
wrong he was to surmise that the knowing nod
of your head meant he had nothing to dread.
You are a saint, Nick,
and I will be waiting for you next Christmas Eve.

Your devoted,
Catherine

P.S. I will put sleeping pills in Clement's eggnog.

My Beautiful Catherine,

I can hardly wait to slide down your chimney!
Ho! Ho! Ho!

Bad Days at Black Rock

A Sestina in Seven Parts

I.

This infected world has released bats
from its belfry, multiplying ten-fold:
China, Italy, Spain, and now us. Shoot!
Make the proverbial sign of the cross
six feet apart in the village square.
Mine shafts are full of dead canaries.

II.

In its battered cage, a timid canary
tries to hide as the tireless cat bats
a captured feather around the square
of carpet it has humped into folds.
It executes another leap, crosses
the space; ball to hoop, itself it shoots.

III.

False spring has coaxed pale shoots
from the warming soil, canary
yellow in their newness, but cross
and cold, it chills little brown bats
that wake too soon, delicate folds
of wing doubled over, death squared.

IV.

Boy Scouts used to pledge, *Be square*,
but the Liar in Chief fires or shoots
down brave sheep that leave his fold.
Contradict him to sing like a canary,
and Cohen goes from first base to bat
boy, testimony called a double cross.

V.

A gambler signs his life away with cross
on dotted line, then throws the square
of paper into oblivion and sees it bat-
flap toward his ruination and shoot
to an unmarked account in the Canary
Islands. Que sera sera; another loser folds.

VI.

It's her last love note, and along the fold
she has written the cryptic, *Cross
your heart and hope...* So, drink canary
wine, sweet and light as a square
of white chocolate. Go the whole shoot.
Covid positive, it's your turn up at bat.

VII.

Hope for a time with canaries safe in the fold,
no more rabid bats circling a broken cross,
meals always square, and guns that don't shoot.

Chocolate Decadence with Vanilla Icing

He called them cream puff swans on chocolate seas
When first he wooed and wowed them to his bed.
Two cherry cheesecakes cheery, creamy— jeez,
His pecan tarts just gobbled all he said.
But culinary metaphors unique
As his should best be saved for special treats.
Like failed meringue that will not hold its peaks,
Two two-timed women seldom remain sweet.
Especially since these ladies were best friends
And always shared what ardent lovers said.
So once found out, he could not make amends
Since both his sweetie pies wished he were dead.
Then burning cognac of flambé did bode
That just desserts aren't served up al a mode.

ON tHE RiGhT FoOt

Child-free

> A Golden Shovel from Gwendolyn Brooks' *The Mother*

Now beyond a decade since the change, I
still possess a fertile mind and heart, have
no regrets for choosing heartbeats heard
and sleepy head against a lover's chest in
easy love. Fulfilled, I freely sacrificed the
fertile eggs while other women's voices
cooed to children, crooned sweet songs of
Bye o' Baby Bunting ilk, and welcomed the
sexless love of motherhood, still as wind
that does not gust and fails to spawn the
hurricane of carnal joy. No lustless voices
hailed me, and all was well when blood of
monthly flow ran thick and clotted down my
thigh. Intent that prospects should not dim,
my Dalkon shield protected as it killed
the eggs that could have been my children.

When I Becomes We

My voice drowns in the collective voice
of hundreds of thousands of Americans chanting,
"Welcome to your first day; we will not go away."
We cheer when we pass a young man with a sign
that says, "I am a Syrian refugee; I love America,"
and nod to acknowledge the elderly couple
holding a Star of David and placard that says,
"We Remember."

The sea of our humanity swirls in whirlpools
of marchers spilling onto side streets and flowing
off them, streams of single-minded people
clutching hands to keep from losing each other
at intersections along Pennsylvania Avenue.

"Tell me what democracy looks like;
this is what democracy looks like!"

A torrent of booing floods the street
as we pass The Trump Hotel, and cheers rise
as our first wave reaches the dam of roadblocks
that keeps us away from our White House.
We have arrived, and the acclamation rushes
through us, surging through more than a mile
of marchers until 480,000 voices meld into a roar.

Then we squeeze into metro cars, six bodies
in spaces big enough for two, our breasts pressed
against backs of strangers whose breasts press
other strangers' backs.

There is no room to breathe, but we are breathing,
all reassuring each other that we are all right.
And supported by each other, we are all right.

Writing a Poem About Ukraine

I dream that I am
in the hall outside my classroom
in a huddled group of girls
holding a small white rabbit
struggling to breathe.
I cradle it in cupped hands;
it has been torn by talons or teeth.
The broken body stiffens.
"We're losing him," I say.
"Do you want to say goodbye?"
The girls remain calm.
They expect no miracles.
One bends to kiss the little rabbit.
One whispers, "I'll see you soon."

One whispers, "I'll see you soon."
One bends to kiss the little rabbit.
They expect no miracles.
The girls remain calm.
"Do you want to say goodbye?
We're losing him," I say.
The broken body stiffens.
It has been torn by talons or teeth.
I cradle it in cupped hands,
struggling to breathe,
holding a small white rabbit
in a huddled group of girls
in the hall outside my classroom.
In the dream, I am
writing a poem about Ukraine.

NASA'S Mars Rover Dead After 15 Years

fifteen years is all we can ask
we should be grateful
but fifteen years gets shorter every dog

Life Expectancy

> In 1864 Juliet the Elephant died at the circus winter camp

A turtle rests on the bottom of Lake Delavan.
It could have seen the dead elephant
falling like Matisse's cut-out of Icarus
through the enormous hole cut in the ice.

It could have seen the dead elephant,
a dark shape surrounded by light,
through the enormous hole cut in the ice,
in frigid water, metabolism drained,

a dark shape surrounded by light
coming to rest in the sand beside it
in frigid water, metabolism drained
as passive sonar bounced shore to shore

coming to rest in the sand beside it,
eyes the size of golf balls,
as passive sonar bounced shore to shore.
Did boys, long-dead, dare each other,

eyes the size of golf balls,
to dive deep and look Death in the eye?
Did boys, long-dead, dare each other
during the decades of decomposition

to dive deep and look Death in the eye,
falling like Matisse's cut-out of Icarus?
During the decades of decomposition,
a turtle rests on the bottom of Lake Delavan.

Every Spring

Toads no bigger than my fingernail
jump along the curb and try
to scale this towering concrete wall.

And every few steps, I bend
to scoop one into my hands
and send it hopping across the lawn.

Don't tell me Mother Nature
wants these little beings to die
unless they can jump high enough.

Don't say that my mercy delays
the evolution of their species
in this man-made world.

I am here now, and so are they.

Cruel and Fair

Beneath the pines, yet still in view,
coyote crouched as hunters do.
Then agitated pheasant flew.

Coyote followed, clutching air,
the bird escaping by a hair.
Our Mother is both cruel and fair.

Charismatic Megafauna

Though charismatic megafauna please:
The golden eagle, panther, polar bear,
I'm thrilled by wind but love a gentle breeze.

The peppering on snow of black snow fleas,
The sudden dart of vole or squirrel or hare,
Though charismatic megafauna please.

When hollyhocks are haloed by wild bees,
A pellet found beneath an owl's lair,
I'm thrilled by wind but love a gentle breeze.

I listen for the song of chickadees,
Look for the nests revealed on branches bare,
Though charismatic megafauna please.

A dew-glazed web that's woven between trees,
A field of fireflies like tiny flares.
I'm thrilled by wind but love a gentle breeze.

Those black dots in the sky are distant geese.
A hummingbird in stasis brushes air.
Though charismatic megafauna please,
I'm thrilled by wind but love a gentle breeze.

Root Growth

I message my sister and tell her I don't try
to start seedlings anymore since they always die
when I take them outside, and she replies,
"Every day look at them and jostle them,
brush your hand over them to give them
the sense of being outside in the wind.
It encourages root growth.
Eventually you can open a window
so they experience real air.
Then they get to go outside for an hour or two.
Eventually you can set them free and let them grow."

My sister has raised two delightful children.
Every day she looked at them and jostled them,
brushed her hand over them to give them
the sense of being outside in the wind.
It encouraged root growth.
Eventually she opened a window
so they experienced real air.
Then they got to go outside for an hour or two.
Eventually she set them free and let them grow.

Now I am sheltering in place far from them.
Every day I look at photos and jostle memories,
brush my hand over them
to give myself the sense
of being outside in the wind.
It encourages root growth.
Eventually I can open a window
and experience real air.
Then I will go outside for an hour or two.
Eventually I will be free and will have grown.

Fragments of History

Desk clerks usually give me rooms that smell
like old bananas, with views of dumpsters,
and windows that won't open or close.

But this evening I have relaxed in a deep
marble tub, put on a thick terry cloth robe,
and am drinking fine wine on the balcony

while I look out over Athens at the Parthenon
towering against the sky and the Running Man
sculpture racing across the boulevard.

Scooters beep between honking cabs that weave
like a yellow snake as they jockey for lanes;
an ambulance screams the import of emergency.

Suddenly, a sandal brushes my shoulder, plunges
past me, and lands on the swimming pool roof,
its body now an artifact destined to remain

where it has fallen like the ruins of the houses
in front of the Acropolis Museum, preserved
under plexiglass, fragments of history.

A Whack Upside the Head

Hit yourself with a shovel,
NASA told the mole InSight
stuck in a hole of its own making
desperate to get free.

NASA told the mole InSight
like a sleeper agent in a tight spot
desperate to get free,
"You're on your own."

Like a sleeper agent in a tight spot
deep undercover,
you're on your own
when the going gets rough.

Deep undercover
stuck in a hole of your own making,
when the going gets rough,
hit yourself with a shovel.

Mantra with Sound Effects

(singing bowl chimes and sings)

There is nothing wrong with my body
that a girdle can't fix,
the sausage-casing, rubber kind that squeeze
flubber back into toothpaste tubes.

(oooh, aaah, deep breath)

There is nothing wrong with my body
that a long-line bra can't fix,
binding the bulge that pops out
of the girdle like frozen milk
pops the top off the jug.

(long slurping sound)

There is nothing wrong with my body
that padding that bra can't fix;
fluffy muffy puffs of cotton
to transform buttermilk pancakes
into succulent cream puffs.

(onomatopoetic Pop)

There is nothing wrong with my body
that support hose cannot fix,
caressing cellulite and pushing varicose veins
back into the yellowed dough
on my corn dog legs.

(painful mmmfff sound)

There is nothing wrong with my body—

(Long pause......chime on singing bowl)

Fundamentals of Acting

"A bowl of oatmeal," I answer
when my acting teacher asks,
"What are you?"
But he is hungry for more
and wants to know the color
of my bowl.
"I don't know," I say.
"Oatmeal can't see; I just feel
the smooth sides of... "
"Of what?" he interrupts.
"Of what is your bowl made?"
"Plastic?" I guess.
I am tired and hung over,
and it seems like a good guess.
But then, out of nowhere,
my muse whacks me
upside the head,
sentience ignites my protoplasm,
and I blurt, "Cheap blue plastic
like cereal box toys!"
I can see a Nabisco spoon man
knifing the air and tell my teacher
that it is diving
toward my gooey gray guts!
"Noooooooo!"
I shriek as I drop
into a writhing, agonized ball.
"Yes!" he shrieks, waving his arms
as if to cast a spell.
"Now bring yourself to life!"
And I feel
the oatmeal that is me morphing
into a swamp creature rising
from my blue lagoon and dragging
itself toward the sleepy town.

Makes or Breaks

Be sure to do Wordle today. Are you KIDDING ME?
                                        Wanda

"Your score on Wordle makes or breaks your day.
It triggers angst or gives you energy."
That's what my hooked-on-Wordle sisters say.

Do I let Wordle mess with me? No way!
I'll never let that silly game decree,
"Your score on Wordle makes or breaks your day!"

But every day they tell me how the gray
squares turn to green with D or E.
That's what my hooked-on-Wordle sisters say.

So I typed in the word *adore* today,
then entered *stein*, then nailed it— *piety!*
Your score on Wordle makes or breaks your day!

My sister Ellen starts with *grace* or *faith*,
but Wanda, using *snafu*, wins in three.
That's what my hooked-on-Wordle sisters say.

Whatever works for them, I guess, but hey,
I got the word in two tries once— Yippee!
Your score on Wordle makes or breaks your day;
that's what my hooked-on-Wordle sisters say.

Perhaps I Should

Perhaps I should let my possessions go,
retaining nothing but my heart-strength, so
I will not have to face the deep despair
that comes with knowing that I cannot care
for all I have as age begins to show.

By giving up my treasures I might grow
to value fewer things, new freedom know.
Mom's bud vase, Grandma's quilt, my teddy bear—
Perhaps I should let my possessions go.

Out on the frozen pond, dry oak leaves blow,
and just as free, in blue sky wings a crow.
A hunting falcon swoops down on a hare
untethered by the trappings that ensnare,
and deer bed down uncovered in the snow.
Perhaps I should let my possessions go.

Hand-Me-Downs

Father's name
Grandma's room
Cousin's clothes
Siblings' womb

I Will Walk in Winter

I will walk in winter
when bears are sleeping
deep in their caves.
I will rush into living,
stride out afield,
my jacket bright
against bare trees and snow.

Oh, winter, sing to me
when shadows blush
with blue-white cold.
Sing while I breathe in
pristine air
from field to pines.

Call back to crows
above the boughs
and join me, fox and doe.
Let eager spring hear
heartbeats in our songs.

About the Author

Joan Wiese Johannes believes Thornton Wilder was right when his Stage Manager in *Our Town* said only poets and saints truly appreciate life while they are living it. Although not a candidate for sainthood, Joan appreciates her life as a poet, and *Lamenting My Failure to Learn How to Tap Dance: And Other Missteps* is her fifth poetry collection. She has also published creative nonfiction, musical compositions for the Native American-style flute, and articles on topics ranging from teaching language arts to catching her first musky. Winner of the 2011 regional poetry award from the Mississippi Valley Poetry Society and the John and Miriam Morris Memorial Chapbook Contest sponsored by the Alabama Poetry Society, Joan has also won and placed in contests sponsored by Wisconsin Fellowship of Poets, Wisconsin Academy of Arts and Letters, *Peninsula Pulse*, *Free Verse*, and *English Journal*. She is a long-time member of Wisconsin Fellowship of Poets and has served as regional vice president and co-chair of the Triad contest, as well as co-editing the 2012 *Wisconsin Poets' Calendar* and the Winter, 2019 issue of *Bramble* with her husband Jeffrey. After teaching English for 34 years, Joan is now happily retired in the village of Port Edwards, WI where she never tires of watching wildlife, including white deer, coyotes, sandhill cranes, turkeys, and an occasional bear in the field behind the house she shares with her husband Jeffrey and their golden retriever Sophie.

www.ingramcontent.com/pod-product-compliance
Lightning Source LLC
Chambersburg PA
CBHW062039120526
44592CB00035B/1532